All animals need places to live. WomWom needs a place with lots of grass.

Some animals can live with
people. WomWom can live
with people. WomWom also
has a safe place with food.

WomWom can live near
people. Most animals need
lots of space. Animals do not
need people.

WomWom lives in a burrow. Wombats need a burrow for shelter. Wombats need a burrow for being safe.

Whales live in the ocean.
Whales need many things to
live. What do you think are
the whale's needs?

Animals need to be safe.
Some animals are safe in
trees. Do you think the bird
is safe?

Animals live in all sorts of places. What animals would live in the rocks?

WomWom needs a safe place to live. Roads are a danger for wild animals. Is WomWom in danger?

Animals need space to live.
WomWom needs lots of
grass to eat. WomWom
needs a big area to live.

WomWom has wallabies
close to the burrow. Where
would the wallaby be safe?

People need to keep wild animals safe. We do this by making parks for wild animals to live. These areas are safe for animals to live.

WomWom needs a wild
place to live. WomWom has
a lot of space to find food.
WomWom can be safe and
grow to be a big wombat.